Saint Ignatius
of Loyola

Leading the Way

Written by Toni Matas

Illustrated by Picanyol

Color by Carlos Rojas

Based on the
Autobiography of Saint Ignatius of Loyola

Pauline
BOOKS & MEDIA
Boston

Library of Congress Cataloging-in-Publication Data

Matas, Toni.
  [Ignasi de Loiola. English]
  Saint Ignatius of Loyola, leading the way / written by Toni Matas ; illustrated by Picanyol ;
color by Carlos Rojas.
       pages cm
  "Based on the Autobiography of Saint Ignatius of Loyola."
  "Translated by Barcelona Multimedia and the Daughters of St. Paul. Originally published in
Catalan by Barcelona Multimedia, AV Pau Casals, 6, 1-1, 08021 Barcelona, Spain"
  ISBN-13: 978-0-8198-7298-2
  ISBN-10: 0-8198-7298-9
  1. Ignatius, of Loyola, Saint, 1491-1556--Juvenile literature. 2. Christian saints--Spain--Biog-
raphy--Juvenile literature. 3. Ignatius, of Loyola, Saint, 1491-1556--Comic books, strips, etc.
4. Christian saints--Spain--Biography--Comic books, strips, etc. 5. Graphic novels. I. Picanyol,
Josep Lluís M., 1948- illustrator. II. Title.
  BX4700.L7M39713 2013
  271'.5302--dc23
  [B]
                                     2013010456

Translated by Barcelona Multimedia and the Daughters of St. Paul

Originally published as *Ignasi de Loiola* in Catalan by Barcelona Multimedia, AV Pau Casals,
6, 1-1, 08021 Barcelona, Spain

Copyright ©, Barcelona Multimedia and Toni Matas, Illustrated by Picanyol

"P" and PAULINE are registered trademarks of the Daughters of St. Paul.

Published by Pauline Books & Media, 50 Saint Pauls Avenue, Boston, MA 02130-3491

Printed in the U.S.A.

LTW VSAUSAPEOILL4-10J13-03338 7298-9

www.pauline.org

Pauline Books & Media is the publishing house of the Daughters of St. Paul, an international
congregation of women religious serving the Church with the communications media.

1 2 3 4 5 6 7 8 9   17 16 15 14 13

✠

Take, Lord, and receive all my liberty,

my memory, my understanding,

and my entire will,

all I have and call my own.

You have given all to me.

To you, Lord, I return it.

Everything is yours;

do with it what you will.

Give me only your love and your grace,

that is enough for me.

—Saint Ignatius of Loyola

THE LORD OF LOYOLA'S SON IGNATIUS, OR IÑIGO AS HE WAS KNOWN, WAS BORN IN 1491 IN AZPEITIA, A TOWN LOCATED IN NORTH CENTRAL SPAIN.

IÑIGO, I BAPTIZE YOU IN THE NAME OF THE FATHER, AND OF THE SON, AND OF THE HOLY SPIRIT.

IÑIGO WAS THE YOUNGEST OF THE LORD OF LOYOLA'S THIRTEEN CHILDREN.

LOOK! THE LITTLEST LOYOLA!

IÑIGO, THIS IRON WILL EVENTUALLY BECOME A SWORD AND GO TO ENGLAND AND FLANDERS WITH OUR BRAVE SOLDIERS . . .

IÑIGO'S MOTHER DIED WHEN HE WAS YOUNG, SO ONE OF HIS SISTERS-IN-LAW HELPED TO RAISE HIM.

LOOK AT OUR COAT OF ARMS, SON. THESE SYMBOLS TELL ABOUT US. THE POT MEANS WE'RE RICH AND POWERFUL. THE WOLVES MEAN WE'RE STRONG, SHREWD SOLDIERS WHO FAITHFULLY SERVE THE KINGS OF CASTILE.

IÑIGO, IT IS TIME FOR YOU TO BEGIN SERVING AT COURT. THE TREASURER OF CASTILE IS A RELATIVE OF OURS. HE WILL WELCOME YOU INTO HIS HOME AS HE WOULD HIS OWN SON. THIS IS A GREAT OPPORTUNITY; THERE YOU MAY EARN A PLACE AT THE ROYAL COURT.

WHEN IÑIGO FIRST ARRIVED IN CASTILE HE WAS SIXTEEN YEARS OLD. HE LIVED THERE FOR OVER TEN YEARS. IN ARÉVALO HE LEARNED HOW TO READ AND WRITE AND ALSO DEVELOPED A TASTE IN MUSIC.

HE WAS A GREAT FAN OF BOOKS ABOUT CHIVALRY AND ROMANCE.

YOUR HIGHNESS, THIS IS THE LORD OF LOYOLA'S SON.

LOYOLA, YOU SAY? HE'LL BE A LOYAL VASSAL AND A PERFECT KNIGHT.

BUT IÑIGO WAS OFTEN RECKLESS AND GOT INTO MANY DISPUTES.

IÑIGO, TAKE SOME ADVICE. LEARN YOUR LESSON BEFORE SOMEONE BREAKS YOUR LEG.

SOME YEARS LATER, THE TREASURER OF CASTILE DIED, LEAVING IÑIGO WITHOUT A PATRON.

IÑIGO, THIS IS ALL I CAN GIVE YOU. GO AND PRESENT YOURSELF TO THE VICEROY OF NAVARRE. PERHAPS HE CAN MAKE USE OF YOU.

IÑIGO WENT AND BECAME ONE OF THE VICEROY'S KNIGHTS. HE TOOK UP ARMS WHENEVER HIS NEW MASTER REQUESTED . . .

. . . AND USED HIS SKILL WITH WORDS TO NEGOTIATE PEACE IN THE TOWNS OF NORTH CENTRAL SPAIN.

IÑIGO IS RESOURCEFUL AND KNOWS MANY THINGS. HE KNOWS HOW TO REACH MEN'S SOULS, ESPECIALLY WHEN IT COMES TO SETTLING DIFFERENCES AND RESOLVING DISAGREEMENTS.

BEFORE SOMEONE BREAKS YOUR LEG WHEN IÑIGO WAS ABOUT THIRTY, HE WAS ASKED TO JOIN THE BATTLE AT THE FORTRESS AT PAMPLONA, WHICH WAS UNDER ATTACK BY THE FRENCH.

WE WILL NOT RETREAT! MEN, LET'S TAKE ARMS AND DEFEND THE CASTLE!

BAOUM!

BOOM!

PAM!

BANG! BANG!

PAM!

BAOUM!

BOOM!

DURING THE BATTLE ÍÑIGO WAS STRUCK BY A CANNONBALL.

ARGH!

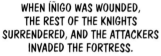

WHEN ÍÑIGO WAS WOUNDED, THE REST OF THE KNIGHTS SURRENDERED, AND THE ATTACKERS INVADED THE FORTRESS.

THE FRENCH TREATED THE WOUNDED ÍÑIGO KINDLY...

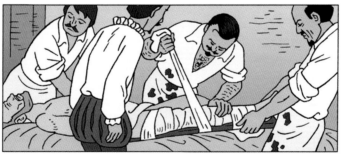

...AND AFTER A FEW DAYS THEY ALLOWED HIM TO BE TAKEN HOME TO RECOVER.

5

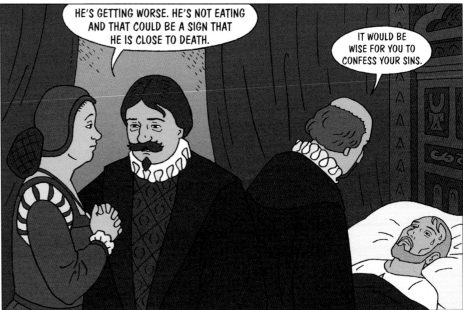

THAT NIGHT SAINT PETER APPEARED TO ÍÑIGO AND HEALED HIM.

HE'S OUT OF DANGER!

A NEW BIRTH

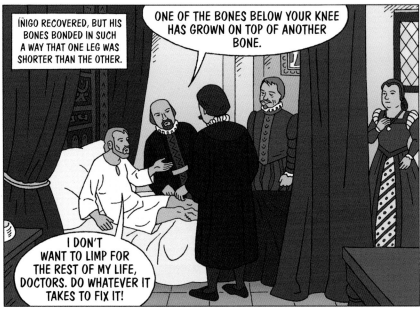

ÍNIGO RECOVERED, BUT HIS BONES BONDED IN SUCH A WAY THAT ONE LEG WAS SHORTER THAN THE OTHER.

ONE OF THE BONES BELOW YOUR KNEE HAS GROWN ON TOP OF ANOTHER BONE.

I DON'T WANT TO LIMP FOR THE REST OF MY LIFE, DOCTORS. DO WHATEVER IT TAKES TO FIX IT!

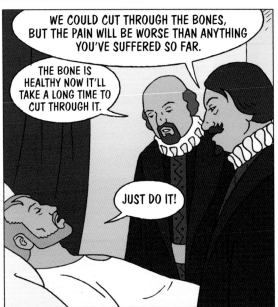

WE COULD CUT THROUGH THE BONES, BUT THE PAIN WILL BE WORSE THAN ANYTHING YOU'VE SUFFERED SO FAR.

THE BONE IS HEALTHY NOW IT'LL TAKE A LONG TIME TO CUT THROUGH IT.

JUST DO IT!

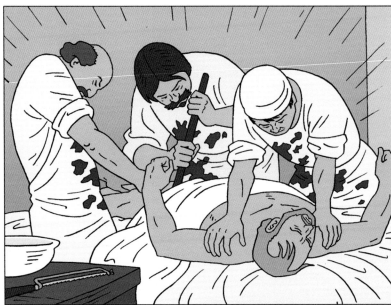

ÍNIGO HAD TO STAY IN BED, BECAUSE ALTHOUGH HE'D RECOVERED, HE COULDN'T PUT ANY WEIGHT ON HIS LEG.

MY SISTER, I FEEL BETTER NOW, BUT I'M BORED. CAN YOU BRING ME SOME EXCITING BOOKS ABOUT KNIGHTS AND CHIVALRY TO READ?

ÍÑIGO DREAMT OF LIVING LIKE THE MEN IN THE BOOKS OF CHIVALRY AND ROMANCE: GOING TO BALLS, FIGHTING WITH SWORDS, AND WINNING A FAIR LADY'S HAND.

I COULDN'T FIND ANY OF THE BOOKS YOU WANTED, BUT I BROUGHT YOU ONE ON THE LIFE OF CHRIST AND ONE ON THE LIVES OF THE SAINTS.

I WONDER WHAT WOULD HAPPEN IF I LIVED LIKE SAINT DOMINIC LIVED . .

OR IF I LOVED THE POOR THE WAY SAINT FRANCIS DID . . . ?

9

HMM . . . WHEN I THINK ABOUT CHIVALRY AND THE WAYS OF THE WORLD I FEEL HAPPY FOR A MOMENT, BUT AFTERWARDS I FEEL UNFULFILLED AND UNEASY.

WHEN I THINK ABOUT GOD AND BEING LIKE THE SAINTS, THOUGH, I BECOME CALM AND HAPPY.

I WANT TO CHANGE THE WAY I LIVE, NOT JUST GO BACK. I WANT TO BE LIKE THE SAINTS. WHEN I'M BETTER I'LL GO ON A PILGRIMAGE TO JERUSALEM TO PRAY AND BEGIN A NEW LIFE.

ONE NIGHT WHILE ÍÑIGO COULD NOT SLEEP HE HAD A VISION OF MARY HOLDING BABY JESUS. MARY LOOKED AT HIM AND SMILED KINDLY.

ÍÑIGO KNEW THAT FROM THAT MOMENT ON THE BLESSED MOTHER WOULD BE HIS LIFELONG GUIDE, ALWAYS LEADING HIM TO JESUS. HIS LIFE HAD CHANGED FOREVER.

GOD'S LOVE GIVES ME SO MUCH STRENGTH. I WANT TO SERVE HIM.

WHEN IÑIGO WAS WELL ENOUGH, HE DECIDED IT WAS TIME TO SET OFF ON HIS PILGRIMAGE TO JERUSALEM. HE SPOKE ABOUT IT WITH HIS OLDER BROTHER.

THE DUKE OF NÁJERA KNOWS I AM BETTER NOW. SINCE HE IS STILL MY COMMANDING OFFICER, I NEED TO GO AND SEE HIM IN NAVARRETE.

IÑIGO, I BEG YOU, DON'T GO! THINK ABOUT THE WEALTH AND POWER YOU COULD GAIN FOR ALL OF US. DON'T THROW IT ALL AWAY!

PILGRIMAGE TO MONTSERRAT ÍÑIGO SET OFF TO SPEAK WITH THE DUKE. AFTER HE MET WITH THE DUKE, HE PLANNED TO GO TO BARCELONA. FROM THERE HE WOULD SET SAIL FOR ROME SO AS TO OBTAIN THE POPE'S PERMISSION TO MAKE THE PILGRIMAGE TO JERUSALEM.

LET'S STOP AT THE CHAPEL OF OUR LADY OF ARANZAZU TO PRAY FOR THE STRENGTH TO COMPLETE OUR JOURNEY.

IN NAVARRETE, AT THE DUKE OF NÁJERA'S HOUSE . . .

THE DUKE SAYS HE MIGHT NOT BE ROLLING IN MONEY, BUT HE WILL ALWAYS DO WHAT HE CAN FOR A MAN OF LOYOLA.

THE MONEY WILL BE DIVIDED AMONG A NUMBER OF PEOPLE. IN ADDITION, PART OF IT WILL BE USED TO RESTORE A WORN-OUT IMAGE OF THE MOTHER OF GOD.

THE DUKE ALSO WISHES TO OFFER YOU A GOOD POSITION IN RECOGNITION OF YOUR GOOD NAME AND AS A REWARD FOR YOUR SERVICE TO HIM IN THE PAST.

ÍÑIGO, HOWEVER, REFUSED THE POSITION. NO LONGER INTERESTED IN A MILITARY CAREER, HE DECIDED TO GO TO THE MOUNTAIN OF MONTSERRAT TO PRAY AT A BENEDICTINE MONASTERY.

SOME WEEKS LATER . . .

NOW I AM LIVING MY LIFE FOR GOD, AS THE SAINTS DID. ALL I DO IS FOR HIS GLORY. MAY THE BLESSED MOTHER HELP ME TO FOLLOW HER SON ALWAYS.

AS ÍÑIGO TRAVELED HE MET A STRANGER. THE MAN WAS NOT A CHRISTIAN, AND HE SPOKE AGAINST MANY OF THE CATHOLIC CHURCH'S TEACHINGS ABOUT MARY.

I SHOULDN'T HAVE LET HIM SPEAK THAT WAY ABOUT MARY, THE MOTHER OF GOD.

I CAN'T LET HIM GET AWAY WITH IT . . . I MUST DEFEND THE BLESSED VIRGIN! I'LL CATCH UP TO HIM AND STAB HIM FOR WHAT HE SAID!

IS THAT WHAT I SHOULD DO?

I KNOW . . . I'LL LET THE MULE DECIDE WHICH PATH TO FOLLOW. IF THE MULE TAKES THE PATH THE STRANGER TOOK, I'LL SEEK HIM OUT AND STAB HIM. BUT IF THE MULE TAKES THE PATH TO MONTSERRAT, THEN I'LL TRUST THAT GOD WANTS ME TO LET HIM GO UNHARMED.

THE MULE TOOK THE OTHER PATH AND ÍÑIGO CONTINUED TOWARDS MONTSERRAT.

WHEN HE REACHED THE TOWN JUST BEFORE MONTSERRAT, HE BOUGHT SIMPLE FABRIC. THIS IS WHAT HE PLANNED TO WEAR ON HIS PILGRIMAGE TO JERUSALEM.

JUST AS KNIGHTS HAVE ALWAYS DONE, ON MONTSERRAT I'LL KEEP VIGIL WITH MY ARMS BEFORE I DEPART.

ONCE HE HAD REACHED MONTSERRAT, HE PRAYED . . .

. . . AND WROTE OUT HIS CONFESSION FOR THREE DAYS.

CONFESSING ALL HIS SINS, ÍÑIGO TOLD THE PRIEST THAT HE NOW WANTED TO BECOME A KNIGHT OF CHRIST.

IF I AM A KNIGHT OF CHRIST THEN I WILL WEAR HIS ARMS. I CANNOT WEAR MY OLD CLOTHES ANYMORE.

ON THE EVENING OF MARCH 24, THE EVE OF THE FEAST OF THE ANNUNCIATION, IÑIGO TURNED OVER ALL HIS FINE CLOTHING AND WEAPONS AND OFFERED HIMSELF TO THE MOTHER OF GOD AS A GENTLE PILGRIM AND FOLLOWER OF CHRIST.

WITH OPEN EYES DRESSED AS A HUMBLE BEGGAR, ÍÑIGO LEFT MONTSERRAT. POSTPONING HIS TRIP TO JERUSALEM, HE HEADED TOWARDS THE TOWN OF MANRESA CARRYING A WALKING STICK AND A SACK. THERE HE WOULD SERVE THE POOR AND SICK.

WE'VE CAPTURED A PAUPER WHO STOLE SOME CLOTHES. HE CLAIMS YOU GAVE THEM TO HIM.

I DID.

ALTHOUGH HIS LEG STILL HURT, ÍÑIGO WALKED ALL THE WAY TO MANRESA USING THE STAFF TO SUPPORT HIM.

LOOK AT HIM!

WITH GREAT TENDERNESS ÍÑIGO WASHED AND CARED FOR THOSE WITH VARIOUS AILMENTS.

HE SPENT MUCH TIME IN PRAYER, ASKING GOD TO FORGIVE HIM FOR HIS PAST SINS.

THE PEOPLE OF MANRESA KNEW HIM WELL. HE WOULD BEG AT DOORS FOR ALMS AND FOOD AND THEN DISTRIBUTE THESE TO OTHERS IN NEED.

IÑIGO WAS SO WEAKENED BY ALL HIS PENANCES THAT THE DEVIL WAS ABLE TO PLAGUE HIM WITH SERIOUS DOUBTS.

GOD HASN'T REALLY FORGIVEN ALL YOUR SINS. ALL THE GOOD YOU TRY TO DO IS USELESS!

LEAVE ME ALONE! I DON'T KNOW WHAT TO BELIEVE ANYMORE . . .

IÑIGO GREW MORE AND MORE CONFUSED.

I'VE SINNED SO MUCH IN MY LIFE; DID I CONFESS EVERYTHING?

I AM WORRIED THAT MY CONFESSION AT MONTSERRAT WASN'T GOOD ENOUGH.

IÑIGO, WRITE DOWN EVERYTHING YOU CAN REMEMBER AND THEN CONFESS NO MORE. GOD LOVES YOU AND FORGIVES YOU.

HELP ME, LORD, I HAVE BEEN SUCH A SINFUL MAN!

LORD, IS THERE HOPE FOR ME? TELL ME WHAT TO DO TO BE FORGIVEN . . . I'LL DO WHATEVER IT TAKES!

ÍÑIGO WAS TEMPTED TO END HIS SUFFERING BY THROWING HIMSELF DOWN THE STAIRS.

LORD, I WILL DO NOTHING TO OFFEND YOU!

I DON'T LIKE HOW I HAVE BEEN LIVING AND FEELING LATELY . . . I WANT A CHANGE.

GOD HAS TAUGHT ME THAT THIS FEELING OF DESPAIR DID NOT COME FROM HIM BUT FROM THE EVIL ONE.

ÍÑIGO WENT TO A CAVE IN MANRESA TO PRAY. THERE HIS MIND BEGAN TO BE CLEARED OF HIS CONFUSION.

LOOK, HERE'S THE PILGRIM!

PEOPLE CAME FROM ALL OVER TO HEAR HIM SPEAK.

GOD TREATS ME IN THE SAME WAY A TEACHER TREATS A STUDENT.

NOW ALL I WANT TO TALK ABOUT IS THE HOLY TRINITY.

I SAW IN MY MIND HOW GOD CREATED THE WORLD.

I WAS GIVEN A DEEPER UNDERSTANDING OF JESUS CHRIST IN THE BLESSED SACRAMENT.

BECAUSE OF WHAT I NOW KNOW, I WANT TO DEDICATE MY LIFE TO PRAYER AND TELLING EVERYONE ABOUT GOD AND ALL GOD HAS DONE FOR ME.

HE SPOKE TO ALL THOSE WHO SOUGHT HIM OUT.

ONE DAY AS I WAS SITTING BY A RIVER BANK . . .

MY EYES BEGAN TO SEE WITH FRESH UNDERSTANDING.

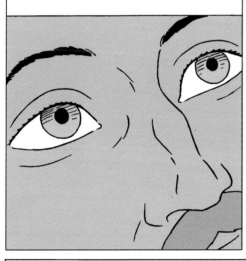

IT'S NOT THAT I HAD A VISION; IT JUST SEEMED THAT I WAS SEEING THINGS FOR THE FIRST TIME.

THANK YOU.

ÍÑIGO WROTE DOWN EVERYTHING HE THOUGHT AND FELT. PART OF WHAT HE WROTE WOULD ONE DAY BECOME HIS FAMOUS WORK, *THE SPIRITUAL EXERCISES.*

IN THE WINTER OF 1522, ÍÑIGO BECAME SERIOUSLY ILL. AFTER HIS RECUPERATION THE WOMEN WHO HAD CARED FOR HIM INSISTED THAT HE WEAR SIMPLE CLOTHING AND A CAP.

THE TIME HAD COME TO SET OUT ON HIS PILGRIMAGE FOR JERUSALEM. FIRST, HOWEVER, HE WOULD TRAVEL TO ROME TO SEEK PERMISSION.

THE SAINTLY MAN IS LEAVING.

PILGRIMMAGE TO JERUSALEM A FEW DAYS LATER ÍÑIGO ARRIVED IN BARCELONA. FROM THERE HE WOULD SET SAIL FOR ROME.

ÍÑIGO, WHILE YOU'RE IN BARCELONA, YOU CAN STAY IN THIS ROOM.

I'VE LOOKED ALL OVER FOR A SPIRITUAL GUIDE, BUT I HAVEN'T FOUND ANYONE WHO COULD HELP ME AS MUCH AS I WOULD HAVE LIKED.

SINCE YOU DON'T HAVE ANY MONEY, I'LL TAKE YOU FOR FREE. BUT YOU ARE RESPONSIBLE FOR BRINGING YOUR OWN FOOD TO EAT DURING THE JOURNEY.

ÍÑIGO, I INSIST THAT YOU TAKE A COMPANION WITH YOU TO ROME. YOU DON'T SPEAK ITALIAN OR LATIN, AND YOU NEED SOMEONE WHO DOES. THAT PERSON WOULD BE OF GREAT HELP.

I WANT GOD TO BE MY ONLY COMPANION. I WON'T TAKE ANYONE ELSE WITH ME.

THE WIND WAS SO STRONG THAT IT TOOK ONLY FIVE DAYS AND NIGHTS TO REACH ITALY.

WE'RE GOING TO ROME TOO. AND LIKE YOU WE HAVE NO MONEY WITH US. MAY WE TRAVEL WITH YOU?

IT WOULD TAKE A FEW DAYS TO REACH ROME SO THE LITTLE GROUP STOPPED TO REST ALONG THE WAY.

COME IN! COME IN!

EAT AND DRINK!

AFTER SUPPER . . .

AAAAH!

HELP!

STOP AT ONCE!

ÍÑIGO FELT THAT IT WAS NOT SAFE FOR THEM TO STAY, AND SO THEY LEFT AND CONTINUED THEIR JOURNEY TO ROME.

SOME DAYS LATER . . .

HERE'S THE POPE'S PERMISSION YOU NEED IN ORDER TO MAKE YOUR PILGRIMAGE TO JERUSALEM.

AND TAKE THIS MONEY. YOU SIMPLY CAN'T TRAVEL FROM HERE TO JERUSALEM WITHOUT MONEY.

I'D RATHER RELY ON GOD THAN ON MONEY. I'LL GIVE IT AWAY TO THE POOR; THEY CAN USE IT MORE . . .

I TRUST GOD WILL PROVIDE THE WAY FOR ME TO GO TO JERUSALEM.

WHAT ARE YOU DOING HERE? WHERE DO YOU WANT TO GO?

I'M A PILGRIM; I WANT TO GO TO JERUSALEM.

THE DUKE OF VENICE CAN HELP. I'LL GET YOU AN AUDIENCE WITH HIM.

THE DUKE ORDERED THAT IÑIGO BE GIVEN PASSAGE ON THE SHIP TAKING THE GOVERNORS TO CYPRUS. FROM THERE HE COULD JOIN OTHER PILGRIMS ON A SHIP TO JERUSALEM.

FROM HERE WE CAN BEGIN TO SEE JERUSALEM. LET'S STOP, CLEAR OUR CONSCIENCES, AND CONTINUE RIDING IN PRAYERFUL SILENCE.

ON HOLY LAND THE PILGRIMS VISITED ALL THE HOLY SITES AROUND JERUSALEM.

26

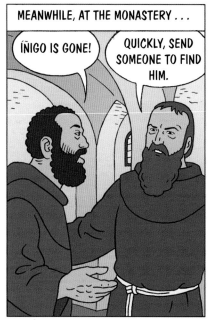

STUDYING IN BARCELONA DURING THE VOYAGE, ÍÑIGO'S DESIRE TO STUDY GREW STRONGER. FROM VENICE HE TOOK ANOTHER SHIP TO BARCELONA.

I BELIEVE GOD WANTS ME TO STUDY.

ÍÑIGO, MASTER ARDÉVOL IS A LATIN GRAMMAR TEACHER. HE HAS VOLUNTEERED TO TEACH YOU LATIN FOR FREE.

AND I CAN PROVIDE WHATEVER ELSE YOU NEED TO LIVE.

WHILE STUDYING, I AM SO DISTRACTED I CAN'T LEARN ANYTHING.

THESE THOUGHTS DON'T BOTHER ME WHEN I'M PRAYING OR ATTENDING MASS . . . ONLY WHEN I TRY TO STUDY.

THEN I REALIZED THAT THOSE THOUGHTS WERE A TEMPTATION TO IGNORE MY STUDIES.

FROM NOW ON I PROMISE I WON'T MISS CLASS ANY MORE. AS LONG AS I CAN FIND BREAD AND WATER TO EAT, I WILL CONTINUE TO STUDY.

LOOK, THIS ONE IS A NOBLE KNIGHT.

HE'S GOT PLENTY OF BREAD.

HERE, MICHAEL, EAT.

GO AWAY, KIDS, LEAVE HIM ALONE!

MOTHER PASQUALA, LET THEM EAT. I WANT THEM TO EAT.

IÑIGO, YOU HAVE MADE THE MOST OUT OF THESE TWO YEARS OF STUDIES. NOW YOU SHOULD GO TO ALCALÁ TO STUDY PHILOSOPHY.

IN JAIL ÍÑIGO ARRIVED IN ALCALÁ AND SUPPORTED HIMSELF BY BEGGING AND LIVING OFF ALMS.

COME AND LIVE AT THE HOSPITAL. YOU'LL HAVE EVERYTHING YOU NEED.

ÍÑIGO STUDIED PHILOSOPHY AND THEOLOGY.

HE SPOKE TO PEOPLE ABOUT THE SPIRITUAL EXERCISES AND HELPED THEM LEARN ABOUT THEIR FAITH.

AT THE TIME, MANY PEOPLE WERE WORRIED ABOUT THOSE WHO MIGHT SPREAD FALSE TEACHINGS.

DO YOU KNOW ANYTHING ABOUT MEN WHO ARE WALKING AROUND TOWN SAYING THEY LIVE LIKE THE APOSTLES?

BE CAREFUL, ÍÑIGO, PEOPLE ARE SAYING THAT YOUR TEACHINGS MAY BE AGAINST THE FAITH!

ÍÑIGO, THE INQUISITORS HAVE BEEN INVESTIGATING YOU.

DID THEY FIND ANY HERESY? HAVE THEY FOUND ERROR IN WHAT WE SAY?

NO. IF THEY HAD, THEY WOULD'VE BURNT YOU AT THE STAKE.

THEY WOULD BURN ANYONE WHO CORRUPTS THE FAITH WITH LIES.

ÍÑIGO AND HIS COMPANIONS KEPT PREACHING AND TEACHING. NO ONE STOPPED THEM.

SOME MONTHS LATER . . .

TOC TOC

COME WITH ME!

YOU WILL STAY HERE IN PRISON UNTIL YOU ARE RELEASED.

THERE IN PRISON, ÍÑIGO TAUGHT THE OTHER PRISONERS.

ÍÑIGO, PLEASE STOP SENDING AWAY THE LAWYERS I SEND YOU. THEY COULD GET YOU OUT OF HERE.

GOD, FOR WHOSE LOVE I AM IMPRISONED, WILL FREE ME WHEN HE WISHES.

YOU ARE HERE BECAUSE A MOTHER AND A DAUGHTER REPORTED THAT YOU TOLD THEM TO ASSIST THE POOR IN DIFFERENT HOSPITALS.

I HAVE COUNSELED THESE WOMEN. I TOLD THEM THAT INSTEAD OF TRAVELING EVERY-WHERE THEY CAN SERVE THE POOR RIGHT HERE IN ALCALÁ.

FINALLY, THE MOTHER AND DAUGHTER, WHO HAD TRAVELED FAR, RETURNED HOME.

WE HAVE DECIDED TO RELEASE YOU. HOWEVER, FOR THE NEXT FOUR YEARS YOU MAY NOT SPEAK OR TEACH ABOUT THE FAITH UNTIL YOU HAVE STUDIED MORE.

ÍÑIGO, FOLLOWING THE ADVICE OF THE ARCHBISHOP OF TOLEDO, MOVED TO SALAMANCA TO STUDY AT THE GREAT UNIVERSITY THERE.

THE PRIESTS AT HOME WOULD LIKE TO SPEAK TO YOU.

I WILL GO AT ONCE.

TELL US WHAT YOU ARE PREACHING.

WE DON'T REALLY PREACH, WE JUST TALK TO PEOPLE ABOUT GOD. WE TALK ABOUT THE DIFFERENT VIRTUES AND HOW TO LIVE THEM. AND WE CONDEMN THE VICES.

MEMBERS OF THE INQUISITION PLACED ÍÑIGO AND HIS COMPANIONS IN JAIL AS THE INQUISITORS STUDIED WHAT HE HAD WRITTEN.

WE HAVE READ WHAT YOU WROTE IN YOUR SPIRITUAL EXERCISES. THERE ARE SOME THINGS THAT CONCERN US. YOU HAVE NOT STUDIED MUCH. PLEASE CLARIFY HOW YOU CAN KNOW THE DIFFERENCE BETWEEN A MORTAL AND A VENIAL SIN.

IF WHAT I HAVE WRITTEN IS TRUE THEN ALLOW IT. IF, HOWEVER, IT IS FALSE, THEN CONDEMN IT.

WHILE THE INQUISITORS CONTINUED TO REVIEW ÍÑIGO'S WRITING, HE AND HIS COMPANIONS WERE HELD PRISONERS.

SOME DAYS LATER, ALL THE PRISONERS ESCAPED FROM PRISON.

IN THE MORNING, ONLY ÍÑIGO AND HIS COMPANIONS REMAINED.

WE HAVE REVIEWED THIS CAREFULLY. WE HAVE FOUND NO FLAW OR ERROR IN YOU OR YOUR WRITINGS. YOU MAY CONTINUE, BUT WE WILL IMPOSE ONE CONDITION: YOU MUST STUDY AT LEAST FOUR MORE YEARS.

LORD, NOW WHAT DO YOU WANT ME TO DO?

I'LL GO TO PARIS TO CONTINUE MY STUDIES.

HE WALKED OVER FIVE HUNDRED MILES FROM BARCELONA TO PARIS, BAREFOOT AND ALONE.

COMPANIONS IÑIGO ARRIVED IN PARIS IN FEBRUARY OF 1528. HE WAS THIRTY-SEVEN YEARS OLD.

WITH THE MONEY SOME FRIENDS HAD GIVEN HIM IN BARCELONA, HE STAYED IN A GUESTHOUSE WITH OTHER SPANIARDS.

HOLD ON TO THESE TWENTY-FIVE GOLD COINS FOR ME.

I'LL CONTINUE MY STUDIES HERE. I'LL HAVE TO STUDY WITH BOYS, BUT FOR THE LOVE OF GOD I WILL DO WHATEVER GOD'S WILL IS FOR ME.

IÑIGO REGISTERED USING HIS LATIN NAME. NOW HE WOULD BE KNOWN AS IGNATIUS OF LOYOLA.

LATER, IGNATIUS WENT TO GET HIS MONEY . . .

I AM SORRY, IÑIGO, BUT I SPENT IT ALL. I HAVE NOTHING TO PAY YOU WITH.

WITH NO MONEY TO PAY FOR SCHOOL, IGNATIUS WENT DOOR TO DOOR BEGGING. HE ALSO HAD NO PLACE TO LIVE.

HE WAS ALLOWED TO STAY AT THE HOSPITAL OF SAINT JACQUES. THIS, HOWEVER, WAS VERY INCONVENIENT BECAUSE HIS COLLEGE WAS FAR FROM THE HOSPITAL. THIS MEANT THAT IGNATIUS MISSED MANY OF HIS CLASSES.

I AM MISSING TOO MANY CLASSES TO MAKE PROGRESS IN MY STUDIES. WHAT SHOULD I DO?

YOU COULD GO ONCE A YEAR TO FLANDERS OR ENGLAND TO BEG AMONG THE SPANISH MERCHANTS. THAT WAY YOU'LL HAVE ENOUGH MONEY TO PAY YOUR EXPENSES FOR THE WHOLE YEAR.

DURING LENT, IN FLANDERS, IGNATIUS MET THE VALENCIAN PHILOSOPHER, LUÍS VIVES.

I LOVE FISH! IT HARDLY SEEMS A PENANCE TO EAT FISH ON MEATLESS FRIDAYS.

I AGREE; FISH IS DELICIOUS. BUT MANY PEOPLE CANNOT AFFORD TO BUY FISH, SO WE SHOULD BE GRATEFUL.

WHEN HE RETURNED FROM FLANDERS TO PARIS, IGNATIUS BEGAN TO GIVE SPIRITUAL RETREATS TO THREE STUDENTS.

THAT SPANIARD WHO SPENT MY MONEY IN FRANCE FELL SERIOUSLY ILL ON THE RETURN TRIP TO SPAIN.

I'LL GO VISIT HIM. MAYBE I CAN HELP HIM PUT LESS IMPORTANCE ON THINGS AND GIVE MORE THOUGHT TO GOD. I'LL LEAVE RIGHT AWAY FOR SPAIN.

I WANT TO SERVE AND LOVE YOU IN ALL THINGS, MY LORD!

IN THE MEANTIME, IN PARIS, THE THREE STUDENTS WHO HAD MADE THE SPIRITUAL EXERCISES GAVE ALL THEY HAD TO THE POOR. LIKE IGNATIUS, THEY BEGGED FOR WHATEVER THEY NEEDED.

THIS CAUSED A GREAT OUTCRY IN THE UNIVERSITY, BECAUSE TWO OF THEM WERE DISTINGUISHED AND FAMOUS MEN.

. . . YOU WILL NOW HAVE TO WAIT TO COMPLETE YOUR STUDIES.

WHEN IGNATIUS RETURNED TO PARIS, HE DISCOVERED THAT BECAUSE OF WHAT HAD HAPPENED WITH THE THREE STUDENTS, A TERRIBLE RUMOR HAD STARTED ABOUT HIM. IT WASN'T LONG BEFORE AN INQUISITOR SUMMONED IGNATIUS.

I HEARD THAT YOU WANT TO SPEAK WITH ME, SO HERE I AM. I WILL DO WHATEVER YOU TELL ME, BUT PLEASE DECIDE QUICKLY SO THAT IT WILL NOT DELAY THE PHILOSOPHY STUDIES I AM ABOUT TO BEGIN.

IT'S TRUE THAT CHARGES WERE BROUGHT AGAINST YOU. BUT AFTER CAREFUL REVIEW I SEE NO REASON TO SUMMON YOU AGAIN.

IGNATIUS BEGAN HIS PHILOSOPHY STUDIES. HE SHARED A ROOM WITH PETER FABER AND FRANCIS XAVIER.

IGNATIUS, I AM SURPRISED THAT YOU ARE NOT SURROUNDED BY PEOPLE LISTENING TO YOU.

THAT'S BECAUSE I HAVEN'T DONE AS MUCH PREACHING AS I USED TO. BUT ONCE I HAVE FINISHED MY STUDIES I WILL BEGIN AGAIN.

EXCUSE ME, DOCTOR . . . I'VE COME TO ASK YOU IF YOU COULD HELP ME FIND A NEW PLACE TO STAY. WHERE I AM NOW MANY PEOPLE HAVE DIED, PROBABLY OF THE PLAGUE.

LET'S GO SEE.

IT'S THE PLAGUE! IT'S SPREADING ALL OVER PARIS!

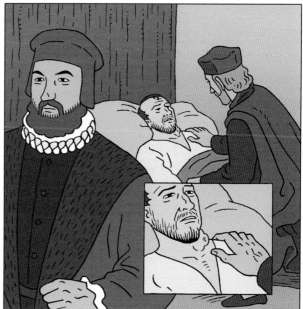

I REFUSE TO GIVE IN TO FEAR OF THE PLAGUE! IT WILL NOT STOP ME FROM DOING GOD'S WORK.

TIME PASSED. IGNATIUS HAD FINISHED HIS PHILOSOPHY STUDIES AND ALSO SPENT SOME YEARS STUDYING THEOLOGY. THERE WERE ALSO OTHER MEN WHO WANTED TO JOIN HIM. AMONG THESE MEN WERE HIS TWO ROOMMATES PETER AND FRANCIS XAVIER.

WHEN WE COULD, WE BROUGHT THE LITTLE WE HAD AND ATE IN ONE OF OUR COMPANIONS' HOMES.

THE FACT THAT WE MET OFTEN AND SUPPORTED ONE ANOTHER HELPED US PERSEVERE.

THE LORD BLESSED US IN OUR STUDIES. HE BLESSED US AS WE CARED FOR OTHERS. AND HE BLESSED US IN THE WAY WE CARED FOR ONE ANOTHER.

MY FRIENDS, TODAY IS THE DAY WHEN WE WILL MAKE OUR VOWS, PROMISING TO GIVE ALL WE HAVE TO GOD.

WE'LL PUT OTHERS FIRST AND IMITATE CHRIST BY LIVING IN STRICT POVERTY.

WE WILL GO ON PILGRIMAGE FROM VENICE TO JERUSALEM AND DEVOTE OUR LIVES TO TAKING CARE OF THE SPIRITUAL NEEDS OF PILGRIMS.

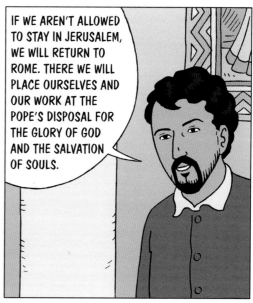

IF WE AREN'T ALLOWED TO STAY IN JERUSALEM, WE WILL RETURN TO ROME. THERE WE WILL PLACE OURSELVES AND OUR WORK AT THE POPE'S DISPOSAL FOR THE GLORY OF GOD AND THE SALVATION OF SOULS.

A YEAR FROM NOW WE WILL MEET IN VENICE TO LEAVE FOR JERUSALEM.

AT THAT TIME, IGNATIUS HAD A SERIOUS STOMACH ILLNESS.

IGNATIUS, WE INSIST THAT YOU SHOULD FOLLOW THE DOCTOR'S ADVICE. HE SAID YOU SHOULD RETURN TO SPAIN BECAUSE THE CLIMATE THERE WOULD HELP TO HEAL YOU.

BUT YOU CAN'T LEAVE YET . . . YOU HAVE BEEN REPORTED TO THE INQUISITOR AGAIN. HE HAS OPENED PROCEEDINGS AGAINST YOU!

IT'S TRUE . . . YOU WERE REPORTED, MASTER IGNATIUS. I HAVE REVIEWED YOUR SPIRITUAL EXERCISES. THEY ARE A GREAT SERVICE TO HELP OTHERS GROW CLOSER TO GOD. IN FACT, I WOULD LIKE A COPY FOR MYSELF.

ONCE THE INQUISITOR'S PROCESS WAS SETTLED, IGNATIUS RETURNED TO SPAIN BY HIMSELF.

BACK HOME AS IGNATIUS APPROACHED HIS HOMETOWN HE DECIDED TO LEAVE THE MAIN ROAD.

I'LL TAKE THIS MOUNTAIN ROAD, EVEN THOUGH IT IS MORE DESERTED AND HAS A REPUTATION FOR ROBBERS. I'D RATHER BE ALONE AS I RIDE.

WHO ARE YOU?

WE ARE YOUR BROTHER'S SERVANTS.

HE SENT US TO ESCORT YOU HOME, TO LOYOLA HOUSE.

PLEASE TELL MY BROTHER THAT I PLAN TO STAY AT THE HOSPITAL FOR THE POOR.

IGNATIUS, YOU CANNOT STAY HERE. YOU MUST COME HOME TO LOYOLA HOUSE.

I'M SORRY, MY BROTHER. I HAVEN'T RETURNED JUST TO LIVE AT LOYOLA HOUSE OR IN SOME PALACE. I HAVE COME TO SPREAD GOD'S WORD AND LOVE.

I'VE DECIDED TO TEACH CHILDREN ABOUT OUR FAITH.

NO ONE WILL COME TO LISTEN TO YOU.

I WILL TEACH EVEN IF IT IS ONLY ONE CHILD.

42

DESPITE WHAT HIS BROTHER SAID, MANY CHILDREN AND ADULTS GATHERED TO HEAR IGNATIUS TEACH AND PREACH.

BECAUSE OF HIS TEACHINGS, THINGS BEGAN TO CHANGE . . .

LOVE THE LORD ABOVE ALL THINGS.

IGNATIUS CONVINCED THE LOCAL JUDGE TO FORBID GAMBLING BECAUSE MANY PEOPLE TRULY NEEDED THE MONEY THEY GAMBLED AWAY.

HE SAW TO IT THAT PUBLIC FUNDS WOULD BE USED TO GIVE THE POOR WHAT THEY NEEDED.

HE ALSO MADE SURE THAT BELLS WERE RUNG THREE TIMES A DAY TO REMIND THE PEOPLE TO PRAY.

BROTHER, I HAVE BEEN PRAYING. NOW THAT I AM HEALTHY AGAIN I BELIEVE IT'S TIME FOR ME TO LEAVE. IF I STAY HERE I WON'T BE ABLE TO SERVE THE LORD AS HE WISHES.

WHILE HE HAD BEEN IN SPAIN, THE NUMBER OF MEN WHO WISHED TO FOLLOW IGNATIUS HAD GROWN. HE RETURNED TO ITALY WHERE SOME OF HIS COMPANIONS WOULD JOIN HIM.

ITALY IGNATIUS ARRIVED IN VENICE BEFORE HIS FRIENDS. WHILE HE WAITED FOR THEM, HE LED GROUPS IN HIS SPIRITUAL EXERCISES.

NINE COMPANIONS ARRIVED IN VENICE AT THE BEGINNING OF 1537.

FROM THERE, THEY SPLIT UP TO SERVE THE POOR IN DIFFERENT HOSPITALS.

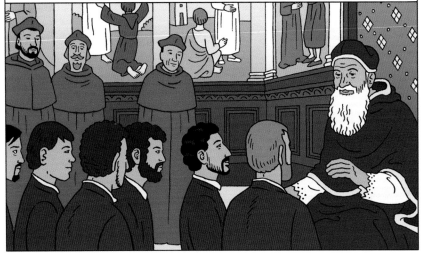

SHORTLY AFTER, SOME OF THE GROUP WENT TO ROME FOR A BLESSING AND PERMISSION TO SET OUT ON A PILGRIMAGE TO JERUSALEM. IGNATIUS DIDN'T GO, HE REMAINED IN VENICE. THE POPE GAVE PERMISSION FOR MANY OF THE GROUP TO BE ORDAINED PRIESTS.

WHEN THEY RETURNED TO VENICE, IGNATIUS AND MANY OF HIS COMPANIONS WERE ORDAINED PRIESTS.

IGNATIUS, WE'RE TOLD THAT THIS YEAR THE SHIPS WON'T SAIL TO JERUSALEM BECAUSE THE VENETIANS ARE AT WAR WITH THE TURKS. IF THEY TRY TO LEAVE THE HARBOR, THE SHIP WILL BE ATTACKED.

WE'LL WAIT FOR NEXT YEAR. FOR NOW WE WILL SPREAD OUT AND PREACH, TEACH, AND WORK IN HOSPITALS IN OTHER CITIES, AS WE HAVE DONE HERE IN VENICE.

IGNATIUS AND HIS COMPANIONS WENT TO THE NEIGHBORING TOWNS AND CITIES. PETER AND DIEGO WENT TO VICENZA WITH IGNATIUS.

THEY RELIED ON THE CHARITY OF THE TOWNSPEOPLE.

THEY ALSO SPENT FORTY DAYS IN PRAYER. THIS WOULD LATER BECOME THE MODEL OF IGNATIUS'S SPIRITUAL EXERCISES.

JUST AS WE DECIDED, WE'LL SEPARATE AND PREACH TO THE PEOPLE.

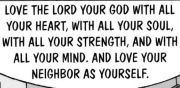

LOVE THE LORD YOUR GOD WITH ALL YOUR HEART, WITH ALL YOUR SOUL, WITH ALL YOUR STRENGTH, AND WITH ALL YOUR MIND. AND LOVE YOUR NEIGHBOR AS YOURSELF.

WHILE FATHER IGNATIUS PREPARED TO CELEBRATE HIS FIRST MASS HE HAD SPIRITUAL VISIONS LIKE THE ONES HE HAD WHEN HE WAS IN MANRESA.

DEAR MARY, MOTHER OF JESUS, HELP ME STAY CLOSE TO YOUR SON.

ONE DAY, WHILE PRAYING AT A SMALL CHAPEL IN LA STORTA –A TOWN A FEW MILES FROM ROME– IGNATIUS HAD ANOTHER VISION . . .

WILL YOU TAKE THIS MAN AS YOUR SERVANT, MY SON?

MY WILL IS THAT YOU SHOULD SERVE US.

GOD HAS MADE IT CLEAR TO ME THAT I AM CALLED TO SERVE HIS SON. THE LAST WORDS I HEARD WERE . .

"I WILL HELP YOU IN ROME."

IN ROME, THE SOCIETY OF JESUS SETTLED INTO A HOUSE THEY CALLED "THE VINEYARD."

IGNATIUS WANTED SO MUCH TO HELP PEOPLE IN THEIR RELATIONSHIP WITH GOD THAT HE GAVE THE SPIRITUAL EXERCISES TO MANY DIFFERENT GROUPS.

HE BELIEVED IN PREACHING NOT ONLY BY WHAT HE SAID BUT ALSO BY WHAT HE DID. WITH THE HELP OF IGNATIUS AND THE SOCIETY OF JESUS, GREAT THINGS WERE DONE IN ROME.

THEY CREATED THE HOUSE OF CATECHUMENS FOR JEWS WHO WANTED TO BECOME CHRISTIANS . . .

THE HOUSE OF SAINT MARTHA FOR YOUNG WOMEN WHO HAD BEEN LIVING ON THE STREETS . . .

AND A HOUSE FOR ORPHANED AND HOMELESS CHILDREN IN ROME WHO HAD LOST THEIR PARENTS BECAUSE OF WAR, PLAGUE, OR FAMINE.

BUT SOME PEOPLE IN ROME CONTINUED TO PERSECUTE IGNATIUS AND THE SOCIETY OF JESUS—UNTIL POPE PAUL III GAVE THEM PERMISSION TO CONTINUE WITH THEIR IMPORTANT WORKS.

. . . YOUR HOLINESS, SINCE WE COULDN'T GO TO JERUSALEM, WE COME TO HUMBLY PLACE OURSELVES AT YOUR DISPOSAL, TO SERVE GOD AND TO HELP SAVE SOULS.

WHY DO YOU WANT TO GO TO JERUSALEM SO MUCH? IF YOU WANT TO SERVE GOD AND HIS CHURCH, THEN ITALY IS AS GOOD A PLACE FOR THAT AS JERUSALEM.

CONCLUSION FOR MANY YEARS FATHER IGNATIUS AND THE SOCIETY OF JESUS WORKED JUST AS POPE PAUL III HAD SUGGESTED. IGNATIUS WAS SIXTY-FOUR YEARS OLD WHEN HE FINISHED DICTATING THE STORY OF HIS LIFE. THE SOCIETY OF JESUS HAD BEEN IN EXISTENCE FOR SIXTEEN YEARS.

FATHER IGNATIUS, NOW THAT YOU'VE FINISHED NARRATING YOUR STORY, I'D LIKE TO KNOW HOW YOU WROTE YOUR SPIRITUAL EXERCISES.

I DIDN'T WRITE THE EXERCISES ALL AT ONCE. WHENEVER I FOUND THINGS THAT I OBSERVED IN MY OWN SOUL AND THOUGHT THEY MIGHT BE HELPFUL TO OTHERS, I WROTE THEM DOWN. THE EXERCISES ARE REALLY MORE OBSERVATIONS OF HOW GOD HAS WORKED IN MY OWN LIFE.

FOR EXAMPLE, SOME PARTS I WROTE BASED ON WHAT I FELT AND THOUGHT WHILE I WAS IN LOYOLA, RECUPERATING AFTER THE CANNONBALL HIT MY LEG.

AND THE CONSTITUTIONS, THE RULE OF LIFE, FOR THE SOCIETY OF JESUS, HOW DID YOU WRITE THEM?

EVERY DAY AS I PREPARED TO CELEBRATE MASS I WOULD OFFER GOD A PARTICULAR TOPIC OR SUBJECT THAT I WANTED GUIDANCE ON. I WOULD PRAY ABOUT IT AND THEN BEGIN MASS.

WHILE CELEBRATING THE MASS, I OFTEN HAD VISIONS THAT WOULD CONFIRM FOR ME GOD'S WILL ON SOME ASPECT OF THE CONSTITUTIONS.

I CAN REMEMBER ALL THIS BECAUSE EVERY DAY I RECORDED WHAT HAPPENED IN MY SOUL. NOW I HAVE EVERYTHING WRITTEN DOWN HERE.

LASTLY, I WOULD LIKE TO SIMPLY TELL YOU THAT THROUGHOUT MY LIFE GOD HAS ALWAYS DIRECTED ME.

AS I HAVE GROWN OLDER I HAVE ALSO GROWN IN MY LOVE FOR GOD. AND IT HAS BECOME EASIER FOR ME TO FIND GOD.

THROUGHOUT MY LIFE, WHENEVER I HAVE SOUGHT GOD, I HAVE FOUND HIM.

IGNATIUS DIED A YEAR LATER IN 1555. HE WAS SIXTY-FIVE YEARS OLD. SAINT IGNATIUS OF LOYOLA, PRAY FOR US THAT WE TOO MAY ALWAYS BE FOLLOWERS OF JESUS.

THE END

51

Afterword

On a few occasions during his life, Saint Ignatius was questioned by Church authorities called *inquisitors*. You may wonder who these people were, and why were they bothering Saint Ignatius. In order to understand the story more fully, we need to know a little history about the Inquisition.

The word "inquisition" comes from the word *inquire*, which means to ask or examine. There were two kinds of inquisitions, the Medieval Inquisition and the Spanish Inquisition. Pope Gregory IX began the Medieval Inquisition in 1231 in Germany—almost 260 years before Ignatius was even born! By 1233, the process had spread to Spain, France, and Italy. What we know as the Spanish Inquisition began in 1480. That is the Inquisition you have read about in *Saint Ignatius, Leading the Way*. The Church ended its Inquisitions in the mid 1800's.

The purpose of the Inquisition was to ensure that people were not teaching or spreading heresy, that is false information about the Catholic faith. Heresy is a serious problem because it leads people away from the faith by misrepresenting the beliefs and teachings of the Church as revealed by God. The Inquisition was originally established to guard Catholics against this danger.

Church officials who did the "questioning" or "examining" were called inquisitors. Throughout most of Europe the inquisitors were under the direct authority of the pope. In Spain, however—where Ignatius lived his early life—the ruling king and queen were in charge of the inquisitors.

When there was uncertainty about the truth of what someone was teaching about the Catholic faith that person could be reported to the Inquisitors. The inquisitors —usually Dominican or Franciscan priests— would then investigate the matter fully, and ask the person in question about what he or she had written or said. The inquisitors and other Church authorities examined these people to protect the faithful from being confused about what the Catholic Church teaches and believes. This is what happened when Saint Ignatius and his companions were questioned about what they had told people about how to know what God wants for them. If the people who were questioned were found to be heretics, they would be turned over to civil authorities for punishment by imprisonment, hefty fines, loss of property, and in a few extreme cases, execution.

Many people consider this time of questionings and punishment a dark period of history for the Church, but this was also a time vastly different from our own. It is possible to recognize that the Inquisition was the Church's way of protecting the people's faith and still disagree with some of the methods that were used to carry out that mission.

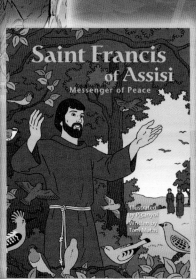

Courage

Commitment

Compassion

These are just some of the qualities
of the saints you'll find in our popular
Encounter the Saints series.
Join Saint Ignatius, Saint Isaac,
Saint Kateri, and many other holy
men and women as they discover
and try to do what God asks of them.
Get swept into the exciting and
inspiring lives of the Church's heroes
and heroines while encountering the
saints in a new and fun way!

Collect all the
Encounter the Saints
books by visiting
www.pauline.org.

ENCOUNTER THE SAINTS SERIES

Saint Isaac Jogues
With Burning Heart
by Christine Virginia
Orfeo, FSP and Mary
Elizabeth Tebo, FSP

Saint Kateri Tekakwitha
Courageous Faith

Adapted from a book
by Lillian M. Fisher

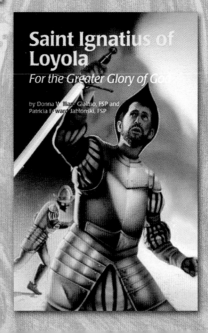

Saint Ignatius of Loyola
For the Greater Glory of God
by Donna William Giaimo, FSP and
Patricia Edward Jablonski, FSP

A Catholic Place for Kids

Your school may have hosted a
JClub Catholic Book Fair.
But did your know that you
can go to

www.jclubcatholic.org

for stories, games, saints,
activities, prayers,
and even jokes!

*JClub is where
faith and fun are friends.*

Who are the Daughters of St. Paul?

We are Catholic sisters. Our mission is to be like Saint Paul and tell everyone about Jesus! There are so many ways for people to communicate with each other. We want to use all of them so everyone will know how much God loves us. We do this by printing books (you're holding one!), making radio shows, singing, helping people at our bookstores, using the internet, and in many other ways.

Visit our Web site at www.pauline.org

Pauline
BOOKS & MEDIA

The Daughters of St. Paul operate book and media centers at the following addresses. Visit, call or write the one nearest you today, or find us at www.pauline.org

CALIFORNIA
3908 Sepulveda Blvd, Culver City, CA 90230   310-397-8676
935 Brewster Avenue, Redwood City, CA 94063   650-369-4230
5945 Balboa Avenue, San Diego, CA 92111   858-565-9181

FLORIDA
145 S.W. 107th Avenue, Miami, FL 33174   305-559-6715

HAWAII
1143 Bishop Street, Honolulu, HI 96813   808-521-2731
Neighbor Islands call: 866-521-2731

ILLINOIS
172 North Michigan Avenue, Chicago, IL 60601   312-346-4228

LOUISIANA
4403 Veterans Memorial Blvd, Metairie, LA 70006   504-887-7631

MASSACHUSETTS
885 Providence Hwy, Dedham, MA 02026   781-326-5385

MISSOURI
9804 Watson Road, St. Louis, MO 63126   314-965-3512

NEW YORK
64 West 38th Street, New York, NY 10018   212-754-1110

PENNSYLVANIA
Philadelphia—relocating   215-676-9494

SOUTH CAROLINA
243 King Street, Charleston, SC 29401   843-577-0175

VIRGINIA
1025 King Street, Alexandria, VA 22314   703-549-3806

CANADA
3022 Dufferin Street, Toronto, ON M6B 3T5   416-781-9131